A Story of Great Light

That Will Make Your Days Bright!

Written by Lois Furtado

Illustrated by Riana Samaroo

WestBow Press books may be ordered through booksellers or by contacting:

WestBow Press
A Division of Thomas Nelson & Zondervan
1663 Liberty Drive
Bloomington, IN 47403
www.westbowpress.com
1 (866) 928-1240

Because of the dynamic nature of the Internet, any web addresses or links contained in this book may have changed since publication and may no longer be valid. The views expressed in this work are solely those of the author and do not necessarily reflect the views of the publisher, and the publisher hereby disclaims any responsibility for them.

Any people depicted in stock imagery provided by Thinkstock are models, and such images are being used for illustrative purposes only.
Certain stock imagery © Thinkstock.

Scripture taken from the King James Version of the Bible.

ISBN: 978-1-4908-5585-1 (sc)
ISBN: 978-1-4908-5584-4 (e)

Library of Congress Control Number: 2014918398

Printed in the United States of America.

WestBow Press rev. date: 11/06/2014

WESTBOW
PRESS
A DIVISION OF THOMAS NELSON
& ZONDERVAN

A Story of Great Light

That Will Make Your Days Bright!

This book is dedicated to my two precious children; Evelyn Sage and Isaac Albert.

Revelation 21:5, "And he that sat upon the throne said, **Behold, I make all things new.** And he said unto me, Write: for these words are true and faithful."

At the very beginning,
God made Adam and Eve.
God told them not to eat a fruit,
and this they did believe.

A serpent whispered a lie,
and the woman was deceived.
Adam and Eve lost their innocence,
and the garden they had to leave.

God trusted a man named Noah,
for he was very good.
And commanded that,
before the waters came,
he build an ark from wood.

After a long time in the ark,
a dove was sent to find land,
not knowing if it could.
After all the days of rain,
it found a seedling with a bud.

As time passed,
the human race behaved badly;
things got worse and worse.
They seemed like they were blinded,
like they were living with a curse.

"We can build a city as high as the
heavens," they proudly said.
So God came down
and changed their speech
and reversed what they had said.

Of all the people in the world,
God chose a faithful man.
To be a father to His people;
He changed his name to Abraham.

God promised his offspring would
multiply, like the stars in the sky.
He finally begot a son named Isaac,
who was the apple of his eye.

Soon after, God's people
were bonded to dire slavery.
So God appointed Moses,
who showed astounding bravery.

Moses cried, "Let my people go!"
But Pharaoh yelled, "No!"
But after ten plagues over Egypt,
Pharaoh told them they must "go!"

God showed tremendous favor
on a small shepherd boy.
He even defeated an angry giant,
with what looked like a toy.

This brave shepherd boy became
an extraordinary king.
He was a great musician and
brought peace when he would sing.

Bad kings after more bad kings,
God's people were getting meaner.
Yet a prophet named Isaiah shared
the hope of their future Redeemer.

A special child would be born,
and He would be known as the
Prince of Peace.
His reign would be never-ending,
and the people's praises
would never cease.

A foreign king commanded worship,
and things became so dire,
That when three men refused to bow,
he threw them in a fire.

"I see four men in the furnace,"
the confused king spoke.
No one perished that day;
they did not even smell of smoke.

God sent His Son, Jesus,
who would be known
as the world-changer.
With no room in an inn,
Jesus was placed
in a wooden manger.

Wise men traveled from afar,
gifting Him with gold,
frankincense, and myrrh.
But He had to escape quickly,
before King Herod found out
where they were.

At a young age, Jesus showed wisdom
beyond anyone's level.
When He was a little older,
He was found tempted by the devil.

"Man shall worship God alone,"
was the statement Jesus made.
He won the fight and passed the test
and angels gave Him aid.

Miracles were done by Him,
and stories He did teach.
Showing men that through His life,
God was in their reach.

Many did follow Him
and saw Him heal and preach.
There were so many people once,
He even spoke upon the beach!

The followers of Jesus were
passionate and zealous.
And all the leaders of the land
became insanely jealous.

Judas had vowed loyalty
that never ceases,
But he betrayed his friend
for 30 silver pieces.

Another criminal that day,
the people had to choose.
Foolishly they freed the guilty one
and killed the King of the Jews.

Jesus died and paid for our sins
on an old rugged cross.
And the hope of our salvation
looked to be forever lost.

Three days later, from the grave,
the Son of God had risen.
He who had no personal sin
could not have death His prison.

For forty days, He appeared to His
people as God's witness.
After all, Jesus was always about
his Father's business.

Thank you, Jesus, Son of God,
for dying in our place,
For tasting death for everyone
and saving every race.

The greatest story ever told
is Your amazing grace.
You now live forever
as the light shines through Your face.

Printed in the United States
By Bookmasters